# GHANA in pictures

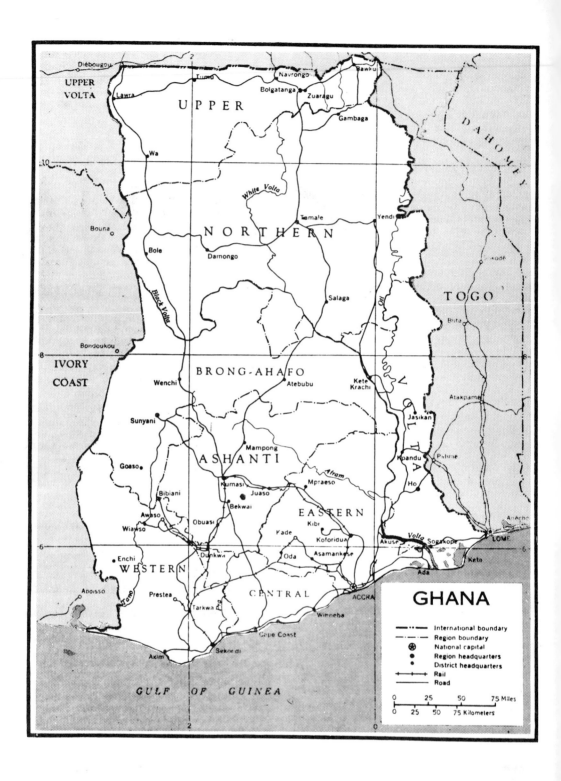

UPPER
VOLTA

Diébougou

Lawra

Tumu

Navrongo

Bawku

Bolgatanga

Zuaragu

UPPER

Gambaga

Wa

DAHOMEY

10

White Volta

NORTHERN

Bouna

Yendi

Temale

Bole

Kodé

Damongo

TOGO

Salaga

Biita

Bondoukou

8

IVORY
COAST

BRONG-AHAFO

Wenchi

Atebubu

Kete
Krachi

Atakpame

Sunyani

Jasikan

V
O
L
T
A

Mampong

Goaso

ASHANTI

Afram

Kpandu

Pahne

Kumasi

Mpraeso

Ho

Bibiani

Juaso

Awaso

Bekwai

EASTERN

Obuasi

Kibi

Wiawso

Kade

Koforidua

Akuse

Volta

Sogakope

LOME

6

Enchi

Dunkwa

Oda

Asamankese

Keta

WESTERN

Ada

Tano

Aprisso

Prestea

CENTRAL

ACCRA

Tarkwa

Winneba

Cape Coast

Axim

Sekordi

GULF   OF   GUINEA

2

0

GHANA

International boundary
Region boundary
National capital
Region headquarters
District headquarters
Rail
Road

0        25        50        75 Miles

0    25    50    75 Kilometers

# GHANA

## in pictures

**Prepared by Lydia Verona Zemba**

VISUAL GEOGRAPHY SERIES

**STERLING** PUBLISHING CO., INC.  NEW YORK

*Oak Tree Press Co., Ltd.*
London & Sydney

# VISUAL GEOGRAPHY SERIES

Afghanistan
Alaska
Argentina
Australia
Austria
Belgium and Luxembourg
Berlin—East and West
Brazil
Bulgaria
Canada
The Caribbean (English-
   Speaking Islands)
Ceylon
Chile
Colombia
Czechoslovakia
Denmark
Ecuador
Egypt
England
Ethiopia

Fiji
Finland
France
French Canada
Ghana
Greece
Guatemala
Guyana
Hawaii
Holland
Honduras
Hong Kong
Hungary
Iceland
India
Indonesia
Iran
Iraq
Ireland
Islands of the
   Mediterranean

Israel
Italy
Jamaica
Japan
Kenya
Korea
Kuwait
Lebanon
Liberia
Malaysia and Singapore
Mexico
Morocco
Nepal
New Zealand
Norway
Pakistan
Panama and the Canal
   Zone
Peru
The Philippines
Poland

Portugal
Puerto Rico
Rumania
Russia
Scotland
South Africa
Spain
Surinam
Sweden
Switzerland
Tahiti and the
   French Islands of
   the Pacific
Taiwan
Tanzania
Thailand
Tunisia
Turkey
Venezuela
Wales
West Germany
Yugoslavia

## ACKNOWLEDGMENTS

The publishers and author wish to thank the Ghana Embassy in Washington, the Ghana Consulate in New York, the Ghana Information Services in Accra, British Overseas Airways Corporation, and the United Nations for the photographs used in this book, and Mr. Adjaye of Ghana Information Services, New York, for his help in the revision.

Sixth Printing, 1973

# CONTENTS

INTRODUCTION ..................................................... 7
1. HISTORY .......................................... 9
2. GOVERNMENT .............................................. 21
3. AREA ............................................. 27
4. THE PEOPLE...................................................... 33
5. ECONOMY AND INDUSTRY............................. 47
6. SOCIAL SERVICES......................................... 59

# INDEX

Aburi, 28
Accra, 7, 9, 10, 27, 30, 31, 38, 43, 45, 53
Accras, 14
Acheampong, Ignatius K., 20, 22
Ada, 30
Adomi Bridge, 47, 55
African professional groups, 15, 16
Aggrey, Dr. J. E. K., 13, 35
Agriculture, 49
AIR SERVICES AND MERCANTILE MARINE, 56
Akans, 10, 11, 33
Akosombo Dam, 53
All-African People's Conference, 24
Almoravids, 10
ANCIENT GHANA, 9, 10
Animism, 45
Ankrah, Lt. Gen. J. A., 20, 24
Arabs, 9, 13
Arden-Clarke, Sir Charles, 17, 18
AREA, 27
Ashanti, 10, 11, 14, 15, 18, 21, 27, 30, 31, 33, 42
Ashanti, King of, 11
Askufo-Addo, Edward, 22
*Atumpan see* talking drum
Bauxite, 52, 53
BEGINNINGS OF BRITISH RULE, 14
Berbers, 10
Berlin Conference of 1884-85, 15
Black Star Line, 56
Bole, 10
Boti, 26
Britain, 7, 8, 12, 14-19, 31, 54
British Commonwealth, 22
British West Africa, 14
Calypso dancing, 40
Cape Coast, 31, 63
Caravan trade, 10
Catholics, 13
Chiefs, 15
Christianity, 13, 14, 54
CITIES, 31
CLOTHES, 35, 38
Cocoa, 19, 30, 48, 49
COLONIZATION OF THE GOLD COAST, 15
COMING OF CHRISTIANITY, 13, 14

Conference of Independent African States, 24
Constitution of 1954, 19
Constitution of 1960, 20
Constitution of 1969, 20
Convention People's Party, 16-19, 21
Coup of February, 1966, 20
Coup of January, 1972, 20, 22
Coussey Committee, 16, 17
Dagarti, 33
Dagomba, 10, 14, 21, 33
Dahomey, 11
Danquah, Dr. J. B., 17
Diseases, 62, 63, 64
DRUMMING AND DANCING, 32, 43
Drums, 32, 39, 43
Durbar, 40, 42
Dutch, 8, 12
ECONOMY AND INDUSTRY, 47-58
EDUCATION, 59-63
Election of 1951, 6, 17, 18
Elmina, 8, 13, 31
EUROPEANS COME TO TRADE, 11, 12
Ewe, 11, 21, 33
Executive Council, 15
FAMILY, 34
Fanti, 10, 14, 21
Federal government, 19
Fernando Po, 49
FISHING, 50
FORESTRY, 51
France, 15
Ga-Adangbe, 11, 33
Gambia, 14
Germany, 15
Ghana Airways, 56
Gold, 11, 12, 52
Gold Coast, 7, 12-16, 18, 27
Gonja, kingdom of, 10
GOVERNMENT, 21-26
Grant, George, 16
Guans, 10
Gulf of Guinea, 27, 29
*Harmattan*, 30
HEALTH, 63, 64
Herodotus, 9
High-life dance, 33, 40
HISTORY, 9-20
History, oral, 9
Illiteracy, 58, 63
INTERNATIONAL AFFAIRS, 24
Ivory, 12, 41, 43
Ivory Coast, 27

Karachi, 10
*Kente* cloth, 35, 36, 38
Keta, 31
Koforidua, 26
Kumasi, 15, 31
Kumasi University of Science and Technology, 63
LAND, THE, 27-30
coastal plain, 27, 30, 31
coastline, 27, 30, 31
forest belt, 27, 30, 31
savannah, 9, 11, 27, 30
Leader of Government Business, 18
Legislative Assembly, 18
Legislative Council, 15
Legon, 63
Livingstone, David, 13
Mali, 27
Mali, Ancient, 10
Mamprussi, kingdom of, 33
March 6, 1957, 7, 9, 19, 21
MINING, 52
Missionaries, 12-14
MODERN GHANA'S ANCESTORS, 10, 11
Moshi, 10
Muslims, 10, 45
National Assembly, 22
NATIONAL CHARACTER, 33
National Liberation Council, 20, 24
National Liberation Movement, 19
National Redemption Council, 22
Nigeria, 11, 14
Nkrumah, Kwame, 16-22
Non-alignment policy, 24
Northern Territories, 6, 10, 14, 15, 17, 18, 27, 31, 33
*Oware*, 39
PEOPLE, THE, 33
Phoenicians, 8
Pliny, 9
Portuguese, 8, 11-13
PORTS, 54
Protestants, 13
Quarshi, Tetteh, 49
Ramadan, feast of, 45
RELIGION, 45
River blindness, 64
Rivers,
Ankobra, 30
Pra, 30
Volta, 28, 30, 53, 55
ROAD AND RAIL, 55

Rubber, 46, 49
Sahara Desert, 9, 27
Salaga, 10
Saltpond, 31
Sekondi-Takoradi, 31
Self-government, 16-18
Sierra Leone, 14
SLAVE TRADE, 9, 10, 12
SLAVE TRADE ABOLISHED, 12, 13
SOCIAL SERVICES, 59-64
Songhay, 10
SPORTS AND ACTIVITIES, 38
STAGE FOUR, 18
STAGE ONE, 15, 16
STAGE THREE, 16
STAGE TWO, 16
STAGES OF DEVELOPMENT IN THE AFRICANS' DESIRE FOR INDEPENDENCE, 15
State trumpeter, 40
Stool, 42
Golden, 10, 11, 15
Sudan, 9, 10
Takoradi, 27, 50, 54
Talking drum, 43
Tamale, 31
Tema, 27, 31, 53, 54
Togo, 27
Togoland, 15
TRADITIONS AND CULTURE, 40-42
Turks, 11
Umbrella, as symbol of Chieftancy, 40
United Gold Coast Convention, 16, 19
United Nations, 19, 24
University College of Science Education, 63
University of Ghana, 7, 63
University of Sankore, 10
Upper Volta, 27, 28
VOLTA RIVER PROJECT, 53, 54
Volta valley, 10, 11
Wa, 29
Watson Commission, 16
"White man's burden," 13
Winneba, 10
WOMEN, 34, 37
World War I, 15

*Voting in the Northern Territories. As a result of national elections held in January, 1951, an African majority was granted, for the first time, a considerable measure of responsibility in the government. Total independence was only six short years away.*

*A chief's representative pours libations in the traditional way on a sacred stone at the opening of a Joint Provincial Council.*

*Student at the University of Ghana.*

# INTRODUCTION

INDEPENDENCE comes but once in a country's lifetime. For that reason March 6, 1957 is a very important date in the history of Ghana. In Ghana this was the day when the British colony of the Gold Coast became the independent and sovereign state of Ghana, and when a colonial legislature was converted into a Dominion parliament.

You can imagine the reaction of the people when they learned that March 6, 1957 was to be the "day of days." A writer from the African magazine, *Drum*, captured the mood best in these words:

> For a moment, until the words registered in the people's minds, there was a deafening silence. Then came the earthquake of emotion that made the sea hesitate from breaking on the beach. That, some say, brought a rain of coconuts tumbling from the trees. That made the very lizards scurry for cover.
> They will tell you the cheers could be heard one hundred miles off. I doubt that. But, apart from the earthquake of 1939, it was without question the most giant explosion of natural or human noise that our ancient land had ever heard.

In the week before independence, people from all corners of the globe and from all occupations in life began to gather in the capital city of Accra. Never in the history of human emancipation had so many contrasting men and women congregated. The variety of their languages was suggestive of a 20th century Tower of Babel. Their complexions were of all shades. But their object in coming was the same—to applaud the birth of a nation.

Ghana was destined to become a symbol for a

*Elmina Castle was built in 1482 by the Portuguese. It was later occupied by the Dutch who sold it to the British in 1872.*

movement which was soon to dominate the entire African scene. A great force was sweeping the continent: it was the determination of the colonial peoples of Africa to govern themselves, to develop their own institutions, and to raise their own standards of living. Most nations of the world have experienced this sentiment. It is sometimes referred to as "nationalism" but it is also recognized as man's desire to be free.

*"Aggrey Beads," once used as money in African trade, are believed to be of Phoenician origin. The seafaring Phoenicians are known to have circumnavigated Africa at the beginning of the 7th century B.C.*

*Ghana's early history can be read in the country's coastline, especially in the line of forts strung along the shore. Through these fortified terminals traders came in and slaves went out. The forts shown in this 18th century print still stand in the middle of Accra.*

# I. HISTORY

ONLY IN recent years have historians paid attention to a history of the Africa which existed before the beginning of European colonization. Africa, except for the ancient civilization of Egypt, was thought to be a great, dark continent. What was the reason? When Europeans first entered Africa, they found the people had no written language, and falsely assumed this meant that Africans had no meaningful history or civilization of their own.

Today we know this was not an accurate picture of Africa's past. Information about early African kingdoms is recorded in the chronicles of such ancient Greek historians as Herodotus, as the Roman historian Pliny, and in the journals of Arab geographers and traders. In addition, modern historians are studying and learning from archaeological discoveries of buildings and artifacts (early original art objects) buried in the African past. They are also talking in African communities with old people who are the safekeepers of an oral history being passed down from generation to generation. It is from various sources—ancient chronicles, archaeological findings, and oral history—that the story of Ghana's past can be told today.

## ANCIENT GHANA

On March 6, 1957 when the former British colony of the Gold Coast became an independent nation, it changed its name to Ghana. The name change occurred because of associations which the ancestors of some of the people of the area are believed to have had with an earlier empire by that name. The ancient empire lay several hundred miles north of modern Ghana, but today the people of Ghana look back to the ancient Empire of Ghana as their cultural ancestor in the same way that modern Europeans look back to Greece and Rome.

The ancient Empire flourished for about a thousand years (from the 4th to 13th centuries A.D.) in the Western Sudan. The Sudan, meaning "country of the black people," is the name the Arabs gave to the great belt of treeless plains (or savannah) stretching across Africa from the Atlantic Ocean to the Red Sea. North of it lay the Sahara Desert and south of it were tropical forests.

It was in the region of the Sudan that large, well-organized, and predominantly Negro states were established during the period

*The Ashanti say that in the reign of King Osei Tutu in the first years of the 18th century, a tribal priest plucked down from the sky this famous Golden Stool, home of the Ashanti soul and the symbol of their glory. It has a throne of its own, on which it rests sideways.*

North (the Berber Almoravids) against other Muslim sects and pagan groups led to the break-up of the three Sudanic Empires. The trans-Saharan trade, so essential to the economic well-being of these empires, was severely disrupted by the Almoravid outbursts. By the 13th century, the Ghana empire had been destroyed, and by the 16th century, the remaining two African empires were broken up.

The people moved in tribal units from the grasslands of the Sudan to seek shelter in the forest regions of West Africa. In their new homes in the forests, they had to begin practically anew to fashion another civilization. It was while they were in the process of doing this that the sea route to West Africa was discovered by the maritime nations of Europe.

## MODERN GHANA'S ANCESTORS

The movement of peoples from the grasslands of the Sudan to their shelters in the forest regions of West Africa is thought to have extended over a period of several centuries, starting about the middle of the 13th century and continuing up to the early part of the 16th. The people who are thought to have come down from ancient Ghana are the Akans. It is said they came in three separate waves, and formed communities with their own sets of traditions and rules.

The first wave of the Akan peoples were the Guans who came down the Volta valley and in the 13th century were occupying the crescent of land stretching from Bole, through Salaga, Karachi, Accra and as far west as Winneba. The second wave consisted of the Fanti people who occupied most of the southwestern coastal area by the 14th century. The third wave brought down the ancestors of the Ashanti people who occupied the central area of the country.

Several other sets of migrations followed. In the Northern Territories, after the Akans had passed through, the Moshi came down (probably from Mali and Songhay) and established the kingdoms of Mamprussi, Dagomba, and Gonja. These groups brought with them the Muslim religion and influences.

Migrations from eastern Africa into modern

known to us as the Middle Ages. At the height of their power, these states could reasonably be called empires. Three of them stand out in history: Ghana, Mali, and Songhay.

A lavish trans-Saharan caravan trade was a vital element in the development of these states. The towns were great markets for gold and slaves from the forest countries to the south; for salt from the Sahara mines; and for horses, cloth, swords, books, and haberdashery from North Africa, and from Europe. They were also important in the spreading of ideas and education. One can read from the works of Arab historians of the great institutions of learning—particularly about the University of Sankore—which drew students from parts of Northern Africa and even Southern Europe.

The fate of the civilizations built up by these African peoples is a reminder to us of the havoc and destruction that can be visited upon a civilization by war. A series of invasions by a warfaring group of Muslim reformers from the

*The 750,000 Ashanti, who live in that part of Ghana which bears their name, have their own language and still cling to their old culture. They believe that their people came out of a hole in the ground. They still have their hereditary king, Otumfuo the Asantehene, Nana Sir Osei Agyeman Prempeh II, but he is by no means an absolute ruler in modern Ghana. He is, however, the spiritual rallying point of the Ashanti nation, and only less sacred than the Golden Stool. However, not even the Asantehene would dare sit on the Golden Stool.*

Ghana were also taking place at this time—particularly from Dahomey and Nigeria. These brought to the coastal plains and Volta basin the Ga-Adangbe and Ewe peoples.

In most cases these early inhabitants had a system of rule in which the heads and elders of families looked after the affairs of each community. Later on, various communities formed states and elected paramount chiefs. The most highly organized and militaristic of these groups were the Ashanti, a section of the Akan peoples.

## EUROPEANS COME TO TRADE

While there had been European contact with North Africa and the interior savannah lands, most of the West African coast remained unknown to the outside world until the 15th century. Africa did not lie along the main commercial routes, as trade in the early Middle Ages was mainly between Europe and Asia. Towards the end of the 11th century, the trade routes between Europe and Asia were closed by the Seljuk Turks. It became necessary for Europe to find a new route to the East. The first Europeans to lead voyages of exploration along the West African coast were the Portuguese. Later, traders from other European countries followed.

By the middle of the 15th century, the Portuguese began to trade. At first it was mainly in gold dust. The large profits gained by the Portuguese led them to name the coastal territory the Gold Coast. Profits also attracted other European countries, and an active rivalry developed among competing European interests, all of whom wished to keep the trade to themselves.

European forts were built along the coast for carrying on trade, but they were also used for protecting this trade. By the end of the 18th century, there was a long chain of European forts all along the Gold Coast—owned by British, Dutch, Portuguese, Swedish, and Danish traders. The forts often changed hands as the Europeans engaged in bitter struggles with each other. In 1642, the Portuguese were driven out by the Dutch. Then, for some time, the Dutch and English maintained the strongest control of the coastal trade. In time, the Dutch sold out their interests to the British.

## THE SLAVE TRADE

Originally, the Europeans came to trade in gold, ivory, and pepper. But, in the 17th and 18th centuries, with the founding of new settlements in the West Indies and in North and South America, large numbers of slaves were required to cultivate the sugar cane, tobacco, and coffee which could be grown there. European rivalries in the Gold Coast during these centuries were for control of the slave trade.

A triangular system of trade was established: ships brought goods from Europe to sell on the West African coast, took slaves across the Atlantic for sale in the Americas, and finally returned to Europe loaded with American sugar, tobacco, and cotton. The business was profitable to the Africans who sold the slaves, as well as to the European slave traders. Towards the end of the 18th century, a slave bought on the West African coast fetched three times the amount on being landed in America.

The cruelties connected with the slave trade were many. It is estimated that for every thousand slaves landed in America, another thousand died through slave raiding and in the passage across the Atlantic. By the middle of the 18th century, 100,000 slaves were being shipped to America every year. This trade had many far-reaching evil effects, but it particularly reduced the population of the African continent and hindered peaceful trade between Africans and Europeans.

## THE SLAVE TRADE ABOLISHED

Through the work of a number of Christian missionaries, Europe was kept informed of the evils of the slave trade. These men stirred the consciences of the people of Europe and impressed upon them their responsibility for putting an end to the slave trade.

Finally, England abolished the slave trade in 1807 and undertook to prevent other nations from engaging in the trade in British territories. The task was difficult. It required a large number of British ships to patrol the seas. Moreover, the Spanish and Portuguese traders,

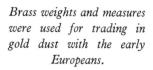

*Brass weights and measures were used for trading in gold dust with the early Europeans.*

along with the African and Arab slave raiders and middlemen, were eager to continue the trade for the profits it brought them. By the middle of the 19th century, the slave trade had been legally abolished by all European countries. In 1863, slavery was prohibited in America.

## THE COMING OF CHRISTIANITY

Although Christian missionaries were present in the Gold Coast after the first Portuguese trading expedition came to Elmina in 1482, their work continued to be of minor significance for some time. However, the 19th century introduced great energy into missionary activity in Africa. It was the century of the "guilty conscience"—guilt, shame, and shock were felt by members of the Christian community that the evils of the slave trade had been allowed to persist so long. It was also the century that rang with the slogan of David Livingstone's appeal that Christians should pick up "the white man's burden" in Africa. A phenomenal number of men and women went to Africa in response to this appeal.

Five major missionary bodies established themselves in the Gold Coast, four of them Protestant and one Catholic. They were the Basel Mission of Switzerland, the Wesleyan Methodist Missionary Society, the North German Missionary Society (Bremen Mission), the African Methodist Episcopal Zion Church (a denomination of American Negro origin), and the Roman Catholic Society of African Missions. These missionaries did not restrict their work to religious conversion. They were dedicated people who contributed greatly to the general progress of the country, in education, health training, child welfare, and scientific cultivation of food. They introduced cash crops, and new industries and occupations. They built and staffed schools, hospitals, and clinics. Some studied the local languages and put them into writing for the first time.

Unfortunately, the good work of the missionaries was sometimes cancelled out by the unfriendly attitudes they held towards other Christian denominations working in the same area. The Africans were not unaware of these

*Dr. J. E. K. Aggrey, one of the founders of Ghana's leading secondary school —Achimota— devoted himself to educating his fellow Africans, and to creating mutual understanding. Emblem of the school was a piano keyboard, which symbolized Aggrey's philosophy: "You can play a tune of sorts using the white keys alone, and a tune of sorts using the black keys alone. But for the best harmony, you must play both the black and white keys." Kwame Nkrumah and many of the ministers in government were students of Aggrey and deeply influenced by his teachings.*

rifts and, in fact, were often encouraged to support the divisions. Missionary influence was also reduced because missionaries often held themselves aloof from personal friendship with Africans. As a result they never learned to appreciate the ceremonies and way of life of the African people. Too many were there to teach and convert, and unwilling to learn. Their ignorance of what was important to the people around them often caused deep resentment in the Africans.

When the church learned of its errors (mostly in the post-World War II period), it began to make amends. An expanded scheme for inviting Africans into the clergy went into effect, and a greater appreciation of the important elements of African culture was introduced.

## THE BEGINNINGS OF BRITISH RULE

At first, English power and influence was limited to the forts along the coast and the ports used by English ships. The English settlers then were interested only in ensuring that protection be given to each settlement and that peaceful trade with the Africans continue. However, in time the responsibility for keeping the peace became too much for the settlers alone.

An African group from the interior, the Ashantis, had organized themselves into a powerful military confederacy. The main cause of their expansionist policy was economic. Their territory (also called Ashanti) was inland country, and European goods were obtainable only at very high prices by way of the coastal Africans—the Fanti and Accras—who served as "middlemen" for the trade. The Ashantis wanted to conquer the coastal African peoples and in this way establish direct links with European traders.

Continuous raids on the coastal peoples by the Ashanti soon followed. Protection became expensive. The British Government decided

*The Gold Coast—Ghana's former name— constituted a portion of the British Empire known as "British West Africa" along with Nigeria, Sierra Leone, and Gambia.*

the Gold Coast was more trouble than it was worth and in 1828 Parliament voted to have the forts dismantled and to leave the territory altogether. But the merchants were not ready to cut their losses, and the coastal Africans were fearful of being left to face the Ashantis alone. The British Government accepted their protests and compromised by handing over the administration of their settlements to a committee of three London merchants. The settlements were to be under a Governor and an elected Council. This arrangement laid the foundations of British rule.

*A Dagomba farmer from the Northern Territories.*

14

## COLONIZATION OF THE GOLD COAST

At first, as we saw, British interests in Africa were limited to maintaining a peaceful atmosphere for trade. However, after the Berlin Conference of 1884-85, the European powers took more than a simple trading interest in Africa. A political competition for colonies broke out among the countries in Europe. The British changed policy as well, for they became alarmed at the northward extension of French and German influence into areas of British trading interest. Britain therefore decided to strengthen its claims.

Treaties of protection already existed between English merchants and coastal peoples, but the Governor was still concerned about the Ashantis. In 1896, the British occupied Kumasi, the capital of Ashanti, and declared the territory a Protectorate. But the Ashantis were not to be contained. In 1900, another Ashanti war broke out when the Governor demanded the surrender of the "Golden Stool." Thinking that it, like the throne of England, was a symbol of authority, he wanted to sit upon it in an effort to make clear his rulership over the Ashanti. This was a great cultural insult and it was to result in much bloodshed. To the Ashantis the "Golden Stool" was sacred for it was believed to contain the soul of the Ashanti nation. It was never to be sat upon.

In this last war with the Ashantis, they were severely defeated, and Ashanti was declared a Protectorate. The same year, the Northern Territories was also declared a Protectorate. When after World War I, Britain had been given one-third of the former German colony of Togoland as a mandated territory, the total administrative unit of modern Ghana—consisting of the Gold Coast Colony, Ashanti, Northern Territories and British Togoland—was complete.

## STAGES OF DEVELOPMENT IN THE AFRICANS' DESIRE FOR INDEPENDENCE

The move to an independent Ghana can be viewed in four stages of development:

*Independent Ghana's first commemorative stamp.*

(1) Political protest of the chiefs and African professional group.
(2) Post-World War II events and the political growth of the city white-collar workers.
(3) The stage of national political activity.
(4) Unifying the country for independence.

## STAGE ONE

When the British took over control of the country in the early 20th century they established a form of central government with a Governor to look after the affairs of the country with the assistance of Executive and Legislative Councils. The Executive Council advised the Governor, but up to 1943 it consisted only of European senior officials. The Legislative Council voted taxes and made laws. Both Africans and Europeans were represented in this body, but its members were appointed by the Governor and not elected by the people.

The Chiefs and African professional groups of doctors and lawyers were not satisfied with this system. Two African protest groups were prominent during this stage: one, the Aborigines' Rights Protection Society, which succeeded in increasing the power of the chiefs as the body for stating local opinion; and two, the National Congress of British West Africa, made up of African professional leaders—the doctors and lawyers. This group first opposed the advisory role of the Chiefs, but later worked

*Kwame Nkrumah, born in 1909, the son of a goldsmith in a coastal village, was educated in mission schools, worked his way through Lincoln University and the University of Pennsylvania (in the U.S.) as a sailor and shipyard worker. In England he studied law, economics, and practical politics. He became Ghana's first Prime Minister, and later its President, the undisputed leader of the government and the Convention People's Party until he was ousted on February 24, 1966. He died in exile in 1972.*

with them in order to obtain more control of the Government.

## STAGE TWO

The post-World War II years (1947 and 1948) saw rising discontent and unrest in the country, as in most of Asia and Africa. Discontent arose from the shortage of consumer goods and rising prices; the opposition of farmers to the Government's destruction of cocoa trees infected by a disease; dissatisfaction with conditions at home by ex-servicemen who had acquired more education and new ideas about their rights and privileges; and rising unemployment in the country, particularly among the ex-servicemen. All this discontent helped to fan the agitation for self-government.

A semi-national political body, the United Gold Coast Convention (UGCC) was formed in August, 1947, under the leadership of George Grant and Dr. J. B. Danquah. This body spoke against the Government for failing to deal with the country's difficulties, and asked for self-government for the people. In December of that year, it appointed a young Gold Coast student studying in England—Kwame Nkrumah (pronounced En-kru-mah)—to become its general secretary and to activate the plans of the Party.

Tensions remained strong in the country for some time. Continued high prices led to a boycott of European goods. Rioting and looting in several major cities in the country resulted. Fearful that events were getting out of control, the United Kingdom appointed a Royal Commission (the Watson Commission) to investigate the riots. In a most remarkable gesture for that time, the Commission recommended the granting of more self-government to the people of the Gold Coast. An All-African committee was appointed (Coussey Committee) to determine how best the recommendations of the Watson Commission could be put into effect.

## STAGE THREE

However remarkable the recommendations of the Watson Commission might have been for the time, the pace recommended for the actual achievement of self-determination by the Coussey Committee was not fast enough for some of the people. Before the Coussey Committee finished its work, Kwame Nkrumah left the UGCC. In June, 1949, he formed the Convention People's Party (CPP). The demand of the UGCC was for "self-government in the shortest possible time," but Nkrumah and some of the young men around him were impatient and demanded "Self-Government Now."

Nkrumah, a first-class political party organizer, had personal charm, captivating eloquence, and gifts of leadership which made men follow him. He and other members of the CPP employed all the machinery and methods of political organization and mass communications known in other countries. They penetrated the

*Dr. Nkrumah was still serving a prison sentence for promoting a strike, when he was elected in 1951 and his party gained a clear majority. The Governor released Nkrumah from prison and he was carried by enthusiastic crowds to Christiansborg Castle, where he was asked to form the first Government of African Ministers.*

towns and villages of the country with their political messages. No longer was political activity limited to the professional groups and white-collar workers, and no longer was it concentrated in the coastal towns. For Nkrumah and his party wooed and organized the masses—farmers, fishermen, artisans, women, the youth—from the camel country of the Northern Territories to the fishing villages of the coast. As no earlier political organization in the country could do, the CPP demonstrated that it could rally nation-wide support for a party and its policy.

When immediate self-government did not result from the Coussey Committee's report, Nkrumah ordered his followers to go on a general strike. This happened on January 9, 1950. As a result, he and other CPP leaders were sentenced to imprisonment. While

Nkrumah was in prison a general election was scheduled for February, 1951, as a result of the new constitution which followed the Coussey Report. Nkrumah's party decided to participate in the election, and Nkrumah himself was a candidate for a seat while in jail. The popular support which he had built behind him and the

*Sir Charles Noble Arden-Clarke, the Governor who both imprisoned Nkrumah and released him, and who later worked hand in hand with him in preparing the country for independence. On March 6, 1957, his office was changed to Governor-General, in the first event solemnizing the change from colony to ninth member of the Commonwealth.*

*Because of Dr. Nkrumah's great flair for the dramatic in his political oratory, his countrymen called him "Showboy."*

CPP became immediately apparent in the election results: the CPP won 80 per cent of the seats and Nkrumah himself was elected though still in prison. The Governor, Sir Charles Arden-Clarke, had little choice. He released Nkrumah and asked him to form a government. Nkrumah became Leader of Government Business in the new Legislative Assembly. A major step had been taken in the movement towards self-government, and from this point onward, the striped prison cap became a symbol of the independence struggle and the sacrifice of the leaders for their people.

## STAGE FOUR

By a constitution introduced in April, 1954, the Gold Coast at last received internal self-government. The final stage of complete independence was not far off. During the period 1954-57, the main source of discontent in the country was no longer between its political leaders and the United Kingdom government. Disagreements arose among various political interests within the country itself, and the old ethnic hostilities among the peoples of the Northern Territories, and the Ashanti people and the coastal regions re-asserted themselves. An understanding of these tensions will serve to explain some of the much-criticized strong political steps taken by the Ghana Government towards members of opposition parties, which are described later in the "Government" section.

Ethnic and religious parties developed in the Northern Territories (Muslim Association Party and the Northern People's Party). In

*Ghana's independence on March 6, 1957 made world-wide headline news. Dr. Nkrumah looks over a few clippings.*

Ashanti, the National Liberation Movement (NLM) was launched in September, 1954. Its leadership was composed largely of the founding members of the UGCC who refused to join Nkrumah's party. It presented the strongest and most organized opposition to the CPP. The NLM's immediate purpose was opposition to the government's action of raising the export duty on cocoa without raising the price paid to farmers. (Most of the country's supply of cocoa comes from the Ashanti region.) Later the NLM and the Northern Territories parties added to their policies the issue of federal versus central government for an independent Ghana. This stirred much heated debate throughout the country. It led to outbreaks of violence, especially in Ashanti. The CPP opposed a federal form of government as impracticable and too expensive for a small country—then less than five million inhabitants. Administrative costs alone for the four or five regional divisions proposed would have crippled the country's economy.

Since the political parties were unable to reach any agreement over the constitutional dispute, the Secretary of State for the Colonies, Mr. Lennox-Boyd, announced on May 11, 1956, that independence could be granted to the country only after a general election had been held and a motion for independence passed by a reasonable majority in a newly-elected legislature. This general election resulted in another gigantic victory for the CPP. The British Government therefore announced that independence would be granted and the date was set. The Opposition then dropped its demand for a federal form of government and demanded agreement on the constitution which would come into force upon independence. The United Kingdom proposals kept the idea of a unitary state, as demanded by the CPP, but introduced many safeguards to satisfy the demands of the Opposition parties. With this compromise the way was cleared to the celebration of independence by the whole country on March 6, 1957. This was followed a few days later by the admission of the new country of Ghana as a member of the United Nations.

After independence, the first nine years of Ghana's history were dominated by Dr. Nkrumah. Nkrumah increased his power and eliminated all opposition parties, leaving himself a virtual dictator. He also became quite important in international affairs, and many people thought Ghana would become a shining example of an African nation adjusting itself to independence.

It was not too long, however, before it became clear that Nkrumah was not as neutral as he claimed, and not as honest as he should have been. His stated reasons for his dictatorial conduct convinced some people that he was doing the right thing, but opposition began to build up against him. He began many grandiose "prestige projects" which the country really could not afford. He organized communist-dominated ideological groups to teach young people his philosophy, and he increased the size of the government beyond what was necessary. People felt that their rights as guaranteed by the constitution were not being observed, and that the Nkrumah administration was keeping them

**19**

hungry while the government leaders were getting rich.

The culmination of the unhappiness with Nkrumah and his party was the coup of February 24, 1966, led by Lt. Gen. J. A. Ankrah, second in command of the Ghana Army, while Nkrumah was out of the country. A group of eight military and police officers formed the National Liberation Council with Ankrah as chairman, and this body of men began to rule Ghana by decree. Committees were set up to operate various phases of the government, and many changes were made to save money. Nkrumah and his top assistants had stolen over $500,000,000 from Ghana and left the country nearly bankrupt. Prestige projects were dropped, and the NLC tried to reorganize the economy on a sound footing.

One of the first acts of the National Libera-tion Council was to assign a Legal Committee the job of drawing up a new constitution. Nkrumah had changed the Constitution in 1960 to give himself virtually all the powers of President, Prime Minister, and party head (in a one-party system).

The new Constitution went into effect in August, 1969. The National Liberation Council was dissolved and Ghana returned to civilian rule and democratic procedures.

Unfortunately the financial problems left by Nkrumah were hard to overcome. The new administration set about paying off Nkrumah's debts, and in order to do this had to cut off funds for social and economic improvements. Many Ghanaians were dissatisfied.

In January, 1972, an army officer, Ignatius K. Acheampong, overthrew the democratic régime and established a new dictatorship.

*Nkrumah soon took the initiative in furthering the concept of Pan-Africanism. In April 1958, he convened a Conference of Independent African States.*

*". . . In consequence of this Act, my Government in the United Kingdom has ceased from today to have any authority in Ghana. . . ." Her Royal Highness the Duchess of Kent, representing the Queen, at the State Opening of the First Parliament of Ghana on March 6, 1957.*

# 2. GOVERNMENT

When Ghana became independent, the British Government bequeathed to it a constitution similar to Britain's own parliamentary system. To this it added five regional assemblies, an advisory House of Chiefs for each region, and a guarantee of the office of tribal chiefs. This addition was a compromise to placate the traditional rulers and regions who feared their interests would not be adequately considered in a unitary form of government.

But Nkrumah feared that division would result if the peoples' loyalties were so fragmented. He wanted to convince the people that they were Ghanaians first. Only in a secondary manner were they to think of themselves as Ashanti, Fanti, Dagomba, Ewe, or members of some other tribe. Because the Convention People's Party won a huge majority of the seats in the national and regional assemblies, in time Nkrumah and the CPP were able to alter the constitution in such a way as to set up a strong, centralized government, concentrating a great deal of power in their own hands, and outlawing criticism of government action. Nkrumah did not deny that his actions were strong-handed. In the preface to his autobiography, published in 1957, he provides us with insights into his reasoning:

Even a system based on social justice . . . may need backing up, during the period

KWAME NKRUMAH
FOUNDER OF THE NATION

SEEK YE FIRST THE POLITICAL
KINGDOM AND ALL OTHER THINGS
SHALL BE ADDED UNTO IT

*The inscription on this statue in front of Parliament House is Nkrumah's belief: that strong political organization in Ghana and Africa is a vital prerequisite for future progress.*

Today Ghana is a Republic within the British Commonwealth of Nations. Initially it achieved its independence as a Dominion within the Commonwealth, but as a result of a plebiscite held in 1960, the people decided to become a Republic on July 1 of that year, and elected Dr. Nkrumah as their President.

After the coup in 1966, the 1960 constitution was abandoned and the National Liberation Council ruled Ghana by decree until a new constitution could be drawn up.

In 1969, as provided in the new Constitution, the people elected a National Assembly of 140 members. The Assembly is unicameral (consists of only one house) and its members are elected for five years. The presidential power remained in the hands of an Executive Commission of three men (one of whom had the title of chairman) drawn from the former National Liberation Council. Appointed in 1969, the Executive Commission held office until 1970, when Edward Askufo-Addo was elected president.

Following the coup of 1972, the National Assembly was dissolved and the governmental power passed to a 12-man National Redemption Council, with Colonel Ignatius K. Acheampong as chairman.

following independence, by emergency measures of a totalitarian kind . . . What other countries have taken three hundred or more years to achieve, a once-dependent territory must try to accomplish in a generation, if it is to survive. Unless it is jet-propelled, it will lag behind and thus risk everything for which it has fought.

*Nkrumah becomes a "fallen idol." The statue of Nkrumah in Accra was the target for irate crowds which gathered after his overthrow in February, 1966.*

*Ghana's Ambassador to the United States, M. A. Ribeiro, presented his credentials to the late President John F. Kennedy in the White House on Thursday, April 25, 1963.*

*People in the rural areas of Ghana receive instructions on how to record their votes for the General Election.*

*After the coup of February 24, 1966, Kwame Nkrumah's one-man rule was replaced with the eight-man rule of the National Liberation Council. Until the new constitution was put into effect, these men were responsible for putting Ghana back on its feet economically and running the country smoothly. All eight men were military or police officers, and the Chairman was Lt. Gen. J. A. Ankrah, seated at the head of the table. Each of the officers had charge of a certain sector of the government. Together these men kept the confidence of their countrymen until democratic government could again be established.*

## INTERNATIONAL AFFAIRS

Kwame Nkrumah had stressed the need for Africans to think in terms of Pan-African brotherhood and especially to take practical steps towards the aiding of African states about to become independent. Two principal organizations arose to work towards these goals: the Conference of Independent African States and the All-African People's Conference. The two political groups differed in that the first was a grouping of independent African states, whereas the second grouped political parties and trade unions in both independent and colonial Africa. Ghana played the most im-portant rôle in originally convening both sets of conferences.

Ghana follows a foreign policy of non-alignment in East-West conflicts. This does not mean that Ghana is isolationist. The Ghana Government believes that international blocs and rivalries aggravate and do not solve disputes. Therefore, in the United Nations Ghana has insisted on freedom to judge issues on their merits and to look for solutions that are just and peaceful, irrespective of the Powers involved. In this respect the Ghana Government also concerns itself energetically with United Nations resolutions for disarmament.

Officers and crew of the Ghana Navy stand at attention as the Ghana naval ensign and national flag are hoisted.

Ghana's Ambassador to the United Nations for several years, Alex Quaison-Sackey, shaking hands with the late Secretary-General, Dag Hammarskjöld. Quaison-Sackey was imprisoned after the 1966 coup, but later released.

*Ghana is not mountainous, but there are several waterfalls such as this one at Boti, near Koforidua.*

*Unloading from surf boats at Accra. While many thousands of tons of cargo are landed monthly at Accra, the landing has to be done by surf boats. Takoradi and Tema are Ghana's only deep-water ports.*

# 3. AREA

THE SHAPE of the African continent is similar to the uniquely-shaped ear of Africa's giant, grey elephant. If you pretend you are to travel around this ear in a counter-clockwise direction, you find the Republic of Ghana at the bottom of the ear's bulge. It may be seen as a rectangular tab running from the southern outline some 440 miles to the interior.

Modern Ghana is made up of the former British Crown Colony of the Gold Coast, the inland Protectorates of Ashanti and Northern Territories, and the Trust Territory of British Togoland. The country covers a land area of 91,843 square miles. This is about the same size as the state of Oregon or of England, Wales, and Scotland put together.

Situated on the Gulf of Guinea, Ghana is bordered to the north by the republics of Mali and Upper Volta, to the east by Togo, and to the west by the Ivory Coast.

## THE LAND

Ghana has no great mountain ranges, its highest point being 2,900 feet above sea level. The land falls into four main divisions: The coastline, the coastal plain, the forest belt, and the dry savannah.

*The largest river in Ghana is the Volta, which rises in the Republic of the Upper Volta south of the Sahara Desert.*

*The botanical gardens at Aburi, dating from the 19th century, contain tropical plants from all over the world.*

*The Chief's House at Wa in the grasslands of northern Ghana.*

*Ghana's coastal belt extends for about 270 miles along the Gulf of Guinea.*

The coastline consists mostly of a low, sandy foreshore on which the Atlantic swells and breaks almost unceasingly. This line is broken in the eastern section, near Ada and Keta, where the coastline is studded with lagoons and creeks separated from the sea by a narrow strip of soil (or sand bar).

Behind the sandy shoreline, for some 60 miles, stretches the coastal plain. This is rolling country, covered with scrub and grass, except at the western end where the forest belt comes close to the sea.

The forest belt itself extends northwards along the western border and into the region known as Ashanti. The trees here have great buttresses and grow 200 feet from the forest floor. This is a valuable timber area, and the moist-shady conditions make this excellent cocoa-growing country. (Cocoa is a major export item of the country.)

North of the great forests the land becomes very arid. This is low, open woodland with treeless plains (savannah) and plateaus.

Rivers and streams are plentiful in Ghana; many are seasonal, but the largest rivers, such as the Volta, Pra, and Ankobra and their tributaries, flow throughout the year.

## CLIMATE

The climate of Ghana is tropical, but contrary to popular belief it is neither unreasonably uncomfortable nor unhealthy. It is exceptional for the thermometer to rise above 95°F. or to fall below 65°F. For most of the year, the daily range is from 75-85°. Moreover, there is no great summer heat or humidity.

Further north, in the dry savannah lands of Ghana, conditions are more extreme. Here there is a severe dry season from November to February or March, when the *harmattan* (a dry dust-laden wind) reaches down from its home in the Sahara. During this time gusty winds blow and red dust settles everywhere, while the parched air sucks moisture from the vegetation. Although the entire country experiences the dry season, the coastal area feels it for only two or three weeks, and the sea breezes soften the effects of the heat.

As in all tropical climates, Ghana experiences

*Accra, the capital city of Ghana, is bustling with over 600,000 people.*

*Some of the hilliest country lies in the area surrounding Amedzofe in eastern Ghana.*

rainy seasons. The coast, the coastal plain and the forest area have two rainy seasons: the big rains from April to July and the small rains from September to November. In the North, however, there is only one rainy season from April to September.

## CITIES

Cities have played a romantic rôle for many of the inhabitants of Ghana. They were the hypnotic drawing points for the energetic village youths who decried the restrictions imposed by rural life and who grasped the infinite opportunities for personal advancement in these cosmopolitan areas.

Of all the cities of Ghana, Accra constitutes the metropolis with its history of some 300 years of contact with the European world. It is America's New York City and England's London. Since Accra was the seat of the British colonial administration, it was the first to benefit from the development of administrative buildings, overseas business establishments, broader health and educational facilities. Luxury items from other countries came to Accra first. It was here that an African professional class took root, and began to develop the ideas for political separation from England that eventually led to Ghana's independence. Accra is still the capital city of Ghana, and the key point for all governmental and business activities. It has a teeming population of over 600,000.

About four hours northwest of Accra, over a good asphalt road, you come to Kumasi, the capital of the Ashanti region. The trip is a most entertaining one, for trundling down the highway, loaded with passengers or crops for market, one sees the African-owned trucks (called "mammy wagons") inscribed with their Homeric-styled doleful and humorous sayings such as: "Friends Today—Enemies Tomorrow," "A Beautiful Woman Does Not Stay With One Man," "The Lord Is My Shepherd —I Don't Know Why," "Paddle Your Own Canoe," "Be Honest With Me Dear," and "No Event—No History." Kumasi is a hilly town with about 280,000 inhabitants. It is still the base of the stoolmaking industry and of many Ashanti cultural activities. Even less populated, however, is Tamale, the administrative capital of the Northern Territories.

Going south once more you find the coastal towns of Sekondi-Takoradi, Cape Coast, Elmina, Saltpond, and Keta. It was in these towns that the Europeans first established their trading posts. Today the two port cities which dominate the country's economic activity are Sekondi-Takoradi and Tema where artificial ports have been constructed to handle efficiently the millions of tons of cargo that enter and leave Ghana every year.

*The greatest hustle and bustle in the towns and villages takes place at the markets where the women enjoy a virtual monopoly in the retail trade.*

*The drums provide not only the inspiration for the dance, but the tonal basis of the many languages in Ghana.*

*Horsemen by the thousand participate in ceremonial occasions in the Northern Territories. Over a quarter of the population live in this area and have developed a tradition that combines African and Muslim principles.*

# 4. THE PEOPLE

OVER 9,000,000 people live in Ghana today. This is about the same number that live in the city of New York, or in Scotland and Northern Ireland combined.

Ethnically this population—like that of the United States—is a melting pot representing a wide variety of African peoples, and some Europeans. Within the African group are the Akans, who live in the coastal area and Ashanti region; the Ga-Adangbe and Ewe, who live in the south-east section; and the Mamprusi, Dagomba and Dagarti, who live in the Northern Territories. It may be difficult to understand just how these groups differ. Basically, they vary in the same way as do members of the Anglo-Saxon family—the English, Germans, and Scandinavians. They have separate languages, and their customs, traditions, and national character have unique overtones.

They also take a great personal pride in sustaining these differences. This holds true similarly for the groups that make up Ghanaian society. Each of the peoples has its own main language, and nearly every main language has its assortment of allied dialects. The official language of the country is English, which is taught in all the schools.

## NATIONAL CHARACTER

Visitors to Ghana are immediately struck by the vitality and gaiety of its atmosphere. This is not a "sleepy" tropical country. Activity begins at sunrise, as soon as the cock crows. Most office workers begin the day at 7:30 a.m., and put in a 45-hour work week which includes half a day on Saturday! By 8:00 a.m. conversation, bargaining over wares in the markets, High-life music resounding from car and home radios, drumming, laughter, traffic noises—all combine to create a contagious rhythm which makes you throw a little dance step into your normal gait. Gloomy faces are rare in Ghana. There is always time to laugh.

Warmth and hospitality towards strangers is another hallmark of the Ghana way of life. The stranger to a city who asks the way will usually find himself escorted to his destination, and then taken to be introduced to the family and friends of his guide.

## FAMILY

Everywhere in Ghanaian society there is a heavy accent on the strength of the family tie. The individual is brought up to think of himself always in relation to family. He is taught to behave in a way which would bring increased respect and never disgrace to its members. Co-operation and mutual helpfulness are essential virtues among relatives. Because of this there is no national problem of caring for the old or finding homes for orphaned children. Someone in the family always is available for looking after infirm relatives.

## WOMEN

Women have always played an important rôle in Ghana society. They have long been known for their genius as retail traders. Throughout the country's trading history, they have represented an important economic and political force. The vast majority of these women (affectionately called "Market Women") are illiterate, but their business know-how makes up for what they lack in formal education. Also, their illiteracy is no bar to their knowledge of what is good for their children and dependents, for they spare no efforts to raise the money that will provide the young with a good education.

It is not surprising that in Ghana's expanded education scheme much thought has been given to the educational needs of women. Dr. J. E. K. Aggrey, the most beloved African educationist, keynoted the reason for this when he said: "Educate a man and you educate an individual, but if you educate a woman then you educate a whole family." Today, Dr. Aggrey's assertion has borne fruit, for the new generation of university-trained women—in addition to their rôles as wives and mothers—are playing an important part in the country as doctors,

*Supermarkets provide Ghanaians with easy access to packaged food products.*

*Girls in other parts of the world go to special schools to learn the fine art of balancing objects on the head. In Ghana every child picks it up naturally.*

nurses, teachers, lawyers, politicians, diplomats and in an endless stream of other professional occupations.

## CLOTHES

Western-style suits are the everyday wear of men in the towns. But the graceful and picturesque *kente* cloth is often worn for formal, ceremonial, or evening occasions. *Kente* cloths are hand-woven on narrow looms. The strips are then hand-sewn together to make up the yards of material (6-7 yards) which men drape over themselves in a toga-like manner. Women fashion the cloth in styles most becoming to themselves, but these usually conform to a general pattern of a full-length skirt, a blouse, and a matching stole.

The weaving of *kente* cloth is a very old and delicate art which dates back some 250 years. Each pattern tells a different story, each pattern a different history.

*Regal in bearing, clad in gold and orange kente cloth, the African tribal chief personifies the drama and majesty of Ghana's cultural history.*

*Kente cloth is woven from silk and cotton yarns in long narrow strips on simple looms and stitched together.*

*The attractive designs on these cotton cloths are especially printed for the Ghana market.*

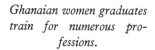
*It is not unusual to see a policewoman directing traffic on Accra's busy streets.*

*Ghanaian women graduates train for numerous professions.*

*The President of the Ghana Women's Council addresses a rally.*

*Boat races in the port of Accra always draw large and enthusiastic crowds.*

Besides *kente* cloth which is quite expensive for everyday wear (a man's toga costs as much as a good suit in England or America, and a woman's as much as a costly dress), gaily printed cotton fabrics are worn. The patterns are designed by artists in Ghana and the fabric is processed in England or Holland. Frequently the patterns are made to pay respect to a particular person or occasion. Brilliant cloths bearing such slogans as "Freedom and Justice," "Stamp Out Illiteracy," or "Ghana Independence Day" give added vitality to the atmosphere of a celebration—or even everyday life.

## SPORTS AND ACTIVITIES

The people of Ghana are keen sports enthusiasts. They are especially fond of soccer and tennis and enjoy watching boxing and wrestling matches. They are active and

*Healthy and strong bodies are important for a developing nation. Soccer and association football teams represent Ghana in international matches.*

*Dancing to the rhythm of drums at festival time.*

successful participants in Olympic and Commonwealth competitions.

An ancient game known as *oware* is also greatly enjoyed throughout the country. Played with palm nuts, dried beans or pebbles, it demands a high standard of lightning-quick mental arithmetic.

No one would dare deny, however, that the most popular relaxation, especially on festive occasions, is drumming and dancing. Ghanaians in the cities, taking the traditional dance steps

*Following the tradition of his family, this elderly drummer has beaten the state drums since he was a boy.*

*These big and heavy drums are called "Fotomfrom" drums. The drum-head marked with a cross is the leader of the orchestra. It dictates the tempo and rhythm of the drum music.*

*The office of state trumpeter is hereditary in most parts of Ghana, and the trumpeters are prominently featured during many festivals. Here one of them blows a ceremonial horn.*

as a basic model, have adapted them and developed an extremely popular and "catchy" dance form called High-life. Today this dance is enjoyed not only in the homes and night-clubs of Ghana, but in the towns up and down the West African coast as well. Similar in tempo to the West Indian calypso (which, by the way, is also derived from the traditional dance steps of Africa), High-life allows each person to interpret his own movements to the music, though always keeping to the one-two beat of the tempo.

## TRADITIONS AND CULTURE

In the years since Ghana achieved independence, many important changes have taken place in the physical appearance of the country: fine new buildings have been erected, new roads span the country, new schools and hospitals have been built, and latest techniques of scientific and industrial knowledge have been learned. But despite all these modern improvements, Ghanaians have made a conscious effort not to destroy the memory of their cultural history.

For this reason the institution of the chieftaincy and the ceremonials attached to it are kept very much alive today. Although the chiefs no longer enjoy the political prestige and power of yesterday, they are the traditional leaders of their people and the safekeepers of their cultural

heritage. Festivals at which the chiefs officiate are still celebrated in Ghana. These are occasions full of the pomp and dignity of centuries; from miles around the people congregate to join in the festivities.

The climax of a festival is generally a *durbar* (a great gathering of sub-chiefs and their

*The umbrella is also a symbol of chieftaincy in Ghana. This carving represents an Ashanti Chief, Queen Mother, and attendants.*

40

*Goldsmiths produce delicate filigree work.*

*Ivory tusks can be transformed into beautiful "jewels" and ornaments.*

*The skill of village women as they shape the river clay without the help of a potter's wheel cannot be rivalled.*

*Notice the unique way in which ceramic ware is used to decorate the outside of this Northern Territories home.*

followers to greet the paramount chief). The *durbar* enables one to see, enjoy, and appreciate at first hand the many aspects of Ghanaian life and culture. A typical *durbar* begins with a formal procession through the town, lasting for perhaps an hour and a half. The lesser chiefs, followed by the paramount chief, ride in palanquins (litters) attended by their retinues and shaded from the sun by large, vivid umbrellas. The rhythm of the umbrellas is an important part of the ceremony: they are made to whirl and cavort in rhythm with the state drums which follow them. At the ceremonial grounds, greetings are exchanged and the state executioners (today purely ceremonial offices) proceed to record with much flourishing of swords the virtues and calamities of old battles. This is followed by an address by the paramount chief to his people, the enjoyment of refreshments, and much drumming and dancing.

*"Stool" means a piece of furniture, but in Ghana it is also a traditional sign of authority. Every Ashanti owns a stool suitable to his or her age, sex, and position. Those of the chiefs are the most elaborate.*

*Carving in wood, ivory and ebony is a time-revered tradition. This ivory and ebony carving shows a man playing on the talking drums.*

## DRUMMING AND DANCING

The most historic and famous object in Ghanaian traditional activities is the drum. It is used on social, military, and political occasions for talking, singing, and dancing. Drumming exists as a true art.

The drum itself is carved from the *kyendur* tree and is usually covered with the skin of a black antelope. The *atumpan* or talking drum, however, is covered with elephant skin.

The talking drum, the most important of all drums, is made up of a pair of drums so big that they must be supported by props. The talking drum is famous for transmitting messages. It was one of the telephone systems of yesterday—and of today as well! Through the traditional proverbs, it speaks in parables. It can roll out the attributes and praises of kings, chiefs, and other individuals on festival occasions. Clever drummers have been known in the far past to incite whole states to take up arms against one another.

To match the drumming, there is the visual delight of the dance. However swiftly the dancers move, however intricate their steps, there is an underlying order in their movements which comes from a perfect sense of timing. Each dancer feels free to add his own subtle interpretation to the dance without detracting from the order of the whole group.

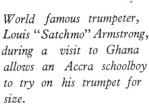

*World famous trumpeter, Louis "Satchmo" Armstrong, during a visit to Ghana allows an Accra schoolboy to try on his trumpet for size.*

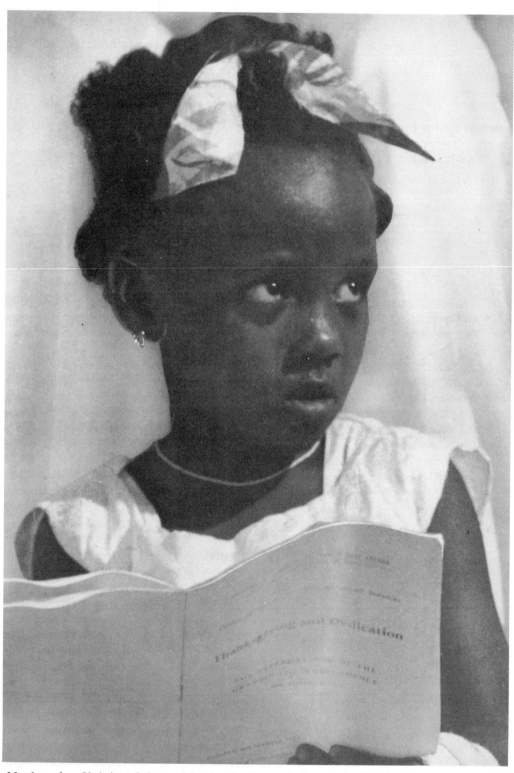

*Member of a Christian choir participating in the pre-independence Thanksgiving and Dedication Ceremony.*

*Anglican Church choristers in procession after Sunday worship in Accra.*

## RELIGION

Towns and villages contain churches of various Christian denominations, mosques, and traditional religious shrines. The major portion of the population—concentrated mostly in the small rural villages—still holds traditional animist beliefs. Christianity (spread by the European missionaries), and Islam (carried down from North Africa), have attracted a great number of followers as well.

It is important not to frown at the words "animist beliefs" or to make snap value judgments about their worth. One must first seek to understand this form of worship and to study its origins. Animists believe that all objects possess a natural life or vitality. These beliefs have existed in pre-scientific societies in many parts of the world, including Europe. They represent the attempts of a people—without the current knowledge of physics, biology, and medicine—to answer questions regarding the nature of the universe, the forces which control it, and the rôle and obligations of man within this picture. Animist explanations led to a rich collection of folklore and folk art, and to orderly political and social systems.

Since pre-scientific societies are mainly agricultural, the lives of the people are especially close to nature. It is not difficult to understand how elements such as the sky, sea, rivers, forests, and the like have been thought to possess separate lives and souls, and have thus assumed human or god-like qualities in the eyes of the people.

In the scientific 20th century many of these early explanations are disappearing because of the strength and influence of education. The strange happenings that occur in the sky, earth, and sea can now be examined and explored according to a logical set of scientific laws. Reform is, therefore, taking place in animists' traditional religious beliefs in somewhat the same way that Judaism and Christianity today are re-examining some of their own ceremonies and assumptions, born in earlier centuries, in an effort to allow their religions to serve better the spiritual needs of 20th-century man.

*An important event is the annual observance of the feast of Ramadan by the Muslim community.*

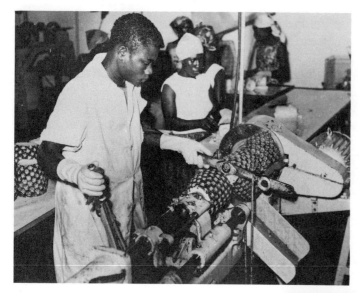

*Pineapples being prepared for canning.*

*Bananas being weighed before shipping.*

*Tapping a rubber tree at the Bunso Agricultural Farm. Although rubber is not a major crop of Ghana at the present time, experiments being conducted at Bunso may lead to its becoming important in the country's economy.*

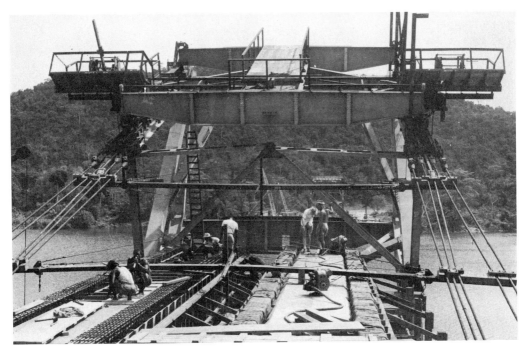

*Workmen fixing the steel reinforcing, ready to pour concrete, to make the approach spans to the main arch of the Adomi Bridge, which links the Volta region with the rest of Ghana. Clearly seen on each side are the ten steel cables, each capable of supporting 100 tons, which are to hold the arch until it is joined in the middle.*

# 5. ECONOMY AND INDUSTRY

ALONG WITH half of the world today, Ghana is regarded as an "underdeveloped," or more properly stated, a "developing" nation. This means that the energies of the people and government are involved in stamping out the unhappiness which results from poverty, illiteracy, and disease; it means that many of the basic services—radio, telephones, roads, electricity, modern transportation, education, medical services—must be built up. It also means that for progress to be made in the shortest possible time, the nation's sources of economic wealth must be developed, expanded, and improved upon.

For this reason in the past 14 years (since internal self-government) a well-planned revolution has been taking place in Ghana's towns and villages, in the welfare of its people, in its institutions, and in its economic capabilities. Much of this has taken place under the organization of two national development plans. These are plans of action for the development of particular industries and utilities, and for production increases within a specific time and within a specific budget.

Much success has been attained in Ghana in the development of new industries. Nevertheless Ghana's economy still depends on its land

*A farmer shows his children healthy pods on a cocoa tree which he planted some years ago.*

*Cocoa trees are sprayed with protective insecticides.*

*Breaking of cocoa pods on a typical farm. After the beans are removed from the pod, they are covered with leaves and allowed to ferment for several days.*

*The cocoa beans are seen here drying in the sun. This takes 6-8 days. During this time they must be raked and turned several times a day.*

and the products that come from it. For that reason agriculture, fishing, forestry, and mining are still the four main props of the economy today.

## AGRICULTURE

The most important crop grown in Ghana is cocoa. Ghana is the world's largest producer of cocoa, and the proceeds from the export of this crop have long been a major source of its wealth. Most of the money spent on development projects in Ghana has come from profits from cocoa.

The story of how cocoa first came into Ghana borders somewhat on the fairy tale with a happy ending. It is said that the first cocoa pods were smuggled into the country in 1879 from the Spanish island of Fernando Po by a Gold Coast blacksmith named Tetteh Quarshie. He planted the blue-green beans at Mampong Akwapim, and four years later, when the trees bore fruit, he distributed pods to his friends and people in the area. Ghana proved to have ideal conditions for cocoa cultivation, and the country has derived great wealth from this simple act of Tetteh Quarshie.

It is dangerous for a country to let one crop control its economics. This is particularly true with a crop such as cocoa, for in some years large numbers of trees are destroyed by a strange virus called "swollen-shoot disease," and other times the rising and falling prices for cocoa on the world market make it difficult for the country's leaders to predict the profits. For this reason, much attention is now given to producing larger quantities of other foodstuffs, such as bananas, coconuts, copra, cola nuts, and tobacco, as well as rubber, palm oil, and many other products.

**49**

*Powered fishing boats at Takoradi.*

## FISHING

For a long time the demands for fish far outweighed the ability of local fishermen to bring in sufficient hauls. This was due to the limitations of the traditional fishing methods. Picturesque and artistic as the gaily-carved and painted fishing canoes may have been, they were just not adequate for large-scale fishing.

Considerable progress has been made to improve the fishing industry. Three objects have been accomplished: small, motorized vessels have been introduced; larger vessels, such as trawlers, are being used; and inland fisheries have been developed.

*Loading a ship by modern means at Takoradi.*

*Traditional fishing boat.*

## FORESTRY

Ghana today has forest reserves totalling some 7,628 square miles. Its forests are an important source of wealth for the export and home markets. For that reason much effort is put into the development of the country's forest estate. These reserves are sometimes used for protective purposes, such as shading for the growing cocoa trees, safeguarding sources of water supplies, and preventing soil erosion. Timber is also used as a main building material, and as a source of domestic fuel.

*In Kumasi, timber is sorted and graded before being shipped by rail to Takoradi for export.*

*Miners in Ghana extract the precious metal which gave the Gold Coast its name.*

## MINING

Large-scale industrial activity in Ghana is concentrated in the mining area. Exports of gold, manganese, diamonds, and bauxite are second only in value to cocoa exports.

Ghana is now the world's second largest producer, measured in carats, of industrial diamonds. Manganese (vital to the manufacture of alloys, especially in the steel industry) and bauxite (used to make aluminium) have also proved highly successful. Gold mining—the country's first and oldest export—has been handicapped because the price of gold has been frozen since 1949.

*The Volta River Project, involving the development of the country's bauxite-aluminium resources by means of a huge dam and hydro-electric power station, was nearing completion in late 1965.*

*Members of the Builders' Brigade—Ghana's domestic Peace Corps—do their morning fitness exercises. A growing nation needs strong and able workers.*

## VOLTA RIVER PROJECT

The most far-reaching of all the industrial schemes is certainly the extensive project on the Volta River. Previously, Ghana had to depend on imported diesel oil for supplies of electricity. For this reason, the Volta River Project, with its production of cheap and plentiful hydro-electric power, is of special importance.

A dam and power station have been built at Akosombo on the Volta to provide electricity for a large-scale bauxite-aluminium industry. A principal consumer of Volta power in the early years is a large new aluminium smelter at the port of Tema. Power is now being transmitted to Accra, the capital city, and a separate ring of transmission lines about 400 miles long now supplies power to towns, villages and mines in southern Ghana.

The $200,000,000 project was financed half by the Ghana Government and half by international loans, especially from the Inter-

*Technical training will provide a strong bulwark to Ghana's industrial growth.*

*View of the new Industrial Development Building (left) and the Ghana Insurance Building in Accra.*

national Bank of Reconstruction and Development and the governments of the United States and Great Britain.

## PORTS

Ghana's coastline has no natural ports. For centuries only surf boats could be used to unload produce from the large freighters anchored out in deep water. These boats were often simple dug-out canoes which were handled with great skill by crews of muscular paddlers, who provided an impressive and hypnotic picture as they swung their curious frog-footed paddles through the huge Atlantic breakers, chanting their uniform motion in chorus.

Today the construction of modern artificial ports at Takoradi and Tema make this cumbersome—though strikingly beautiful—method of unloading unnecessary.

*Stately Ghanaian girl in kente dress. Incidentally, she is a journalist who works at Ghana's Broadcasting Corporation.*

*New-style buses are rapidly replacing the passenger trucks called "mammy wagons." But the custom of attaching names or sayings to the vehicles still survives.*

## ROAD AND RAIL

The expansion of the main road system has been given priority among development projects. Today there are over 5,000 miles of trunk and town roads. In addition a number of road bridges have been built, the largest of which is the 800-foot-long Adomi Bridge over the Volta, completed in 1957. This, one of the largest bridges in Africa, was a major step forward in linking two parts of the country previously connected only by ferry service.

In railways, a number of important links between cities have been established and modernized, and diesel-electric and diesel-hydraulic locomotives are being introduced into the service.

*The Adomi Bridge under construction. It was completed in 1957.*

*Ghana Airways, using the most modern jets, was operated at a loss for "prestige" by Nkrumah, but is now being made into a profitable enterprise.*

## AIR SERVICES
## AND MERCANTILE MARINE

Another sign of Ghana's tremendous rate of progress has been the formation of its own airlines and its own merchant marine fleet. Ghanaian pilots and stewardesses proudly staff the planes of the Ghana Airways system. The Black Star Line, Ghana's merchant marine fleet established in 1958, has already expanded considerably since its formation and is adding regularly to the number of its ships.

## PUBLIC UTILITIES AND PUBLIC WORKS

Water and electricity have both been featured in the national development plans as essential to agricultural and industrial expansion, as well as for the increased health and welfare of the people. The government has been especially concerned about the needs of rural areas and small towns, while at the same time trying to meet the growing urban demands. In a developing nation, demands for improvement come from all parts of society.

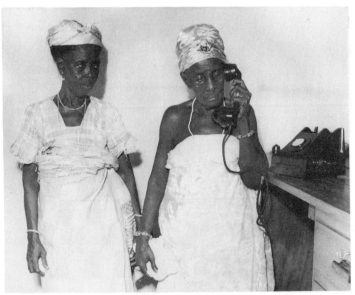

*Not all parts of Ghana have telephone service, but efforts are being made to extend facilities as widely as possible.*

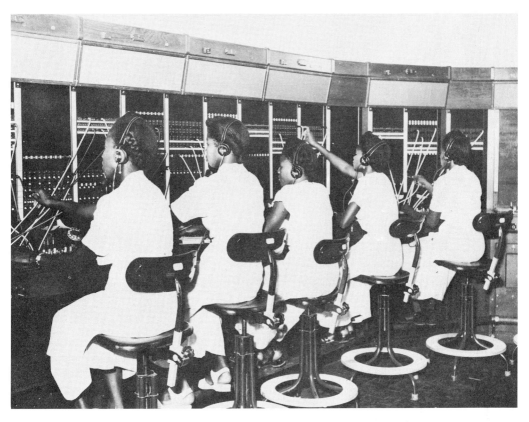

*Operators at work at the automatic telephone exchange in Accra.*

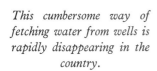

*This cumbersome way of fetching water from wells is rapidly disappearing in the country.*

*Wiping out illiteracy in the villages is a prime task for government social workers.*

*One is never too old to learn to read and write.*

*Ghana's libraries will serve as a repository of the world's knowledge.*

# 6. SOCIAL SERVICES

THE DEVELOPMENT of a country's natural resources is a meaningless exercise if the potentials of the people are not expanded as well. For this reason the Ghana Government views the education and training of its people and the creation of a healthy community as an essential part of all its development planning. A great deal of time and money is set aside for plans in this area.

## EDUCATION

Of all the social services, education is thought to be the most important cure-all to the nation's ills, the most vital to the country's future de-velopment. This desire for more and more education exists not only as part of the government's scheme for the people. It exists also as a fervent desire among the population for their children, family, and selves. It is not uncommon in an African country for a teacher to punish a disobedient child by *forbidding* him to come to school for the next day or two. This is recognized as the most severe penalty any teacher could inflict.

The years since 1951 have brought some of the greatest strides in increased educational opportunity for the people. In 1951, when the first all-African Legislative Council was elected

*Girls' secondary school. Ghana's school-building schedule is ever increasing.*

by the people, it immediately set in motion a new education plan for the country. Under this plan primary education was speeded up, all primary school fees abolished, a vast school-building project started, and teacher-training facilities expanded. Between 1951 and 1959, Ghana spent a very large part of its revenues on education alone. The results of all this expenditure for education were most rewarding. During the same period, enrolment in all educational institutions increased from 281,000 to 663,000; attendance in primary, middle, and secondary schools more than doubled; enrolment in trade and technical schools increased about fivefold; and in teacher-training more than twofold. In 1971, total enrolment was 1,370,000.

*Mobile library units carry books to the rural areas.*

*More and more teachers will be required to meet the nation's unquenchable thirst for education. In this picture, students of the Amedzofe Teacher Training College are shown in the classroom of a primary school taking notes on practical teaching methods.*

*You're never too young to begin training as an athlete.*

*Ghana is developing a corps of competent scientists.*

*A medical field unit at work in a village. These technicians are trained in the diagnosis of certain specific tropical diseases—such as yaws, sleeping-sickness, cerebro-spinal meningitis, and leprosy.*

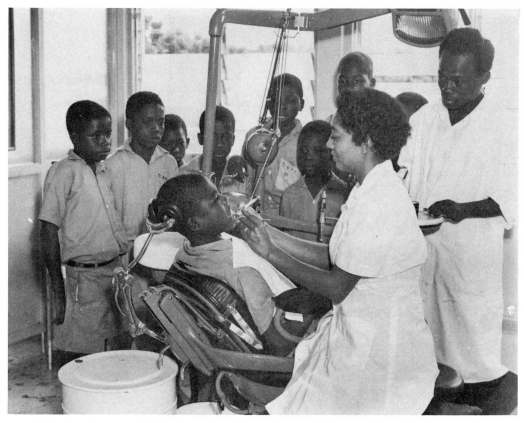

*Dr. S. A. Lee, an American dental surgeon from New York, doing routine checking of school children in a new dental laboratory.*

In addition, Ghana has developed three institutions of higher learning since 1948. These are the University of Ghana at Legon, the Kumasi University of Science and Technology, and the University College of Science Education at Cape Coast. Scholarships were also made available for Ghana students to study abroad.

In addition to education in the regular school system, mass-education campaigns have brought literacy to thousands of adults in rural villages. This is largely the work of the government's Department of Social Welfare and Community Development. Teaching people to read and write is only part of the department's work. It also trains them in home and child care, in village development and it conducts campaigns to improve health, agriculture, and housing in the villages. What is more, the department's staff do not end with just telling the village people how to do things. These technicians live and work in the difficult village conditions along with the people, encouraging, teaching and supervising them.

## HEALTH

There was a time when West Africa had a very sinister reputation in matters of health. It was once called "The White Man's Grave" because a large number of the early explorers and missionaries fell victim to various tropical diseases. Of course, the mortality rate was high for Africans as well, especially for infants. At that time little was known about the cause or cure of tropical diseases. However, modern medical and scientific techniques, developed in the last 40 years, have done much to lessen the occurrence and severity of such diseases as

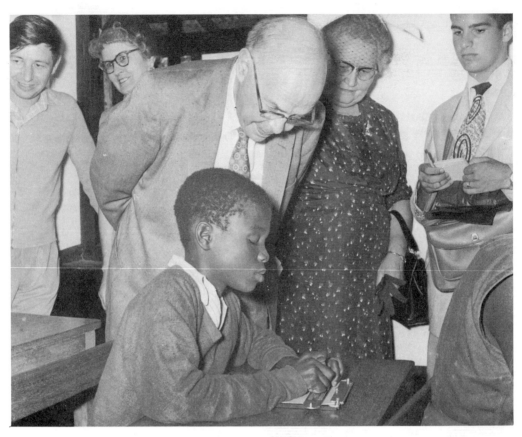

*A blind boy takes down dictation in Braille. River blindness is an endemic disease in Ghana that still requires much study.*

river blindness, sleeping sickness, malaria, yellow fever, and leprosy, which at one time took such a high toll of the population.

Today, the care taken with purifying water supplies and improving standards of sanitation and nutrition is having remarkable effects in reducing infection and raising the general standard of health in the country. An expanding network of hospitals and clinics is also helping to ensure that when disease does occur patients have the benefit of quick and skilled treatment.

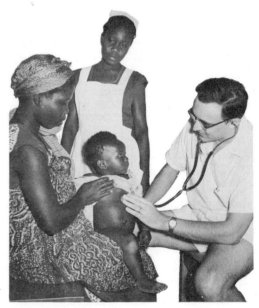

*Health is part of a country's wealth. One of the doctors at Worawora Hospital examines a sick baby.*